MARRIAGE STILL WORKS

MARRIAGE STILL WORKS

*The Five C's to a
Winning Relationship*

PASTOR NELSON WHITE &
AYEISHA WHITE

Black Muse Publishing

Black Muse Publishing
Glodean Champion
5432 Geary Blvd
Unit #621
San Francisco, CA 94121

To request permissions, contact the publisher at publisher@blackmusepublishing.com

ISBN: 9798218210458 (Paperback)

ISBN: 9798218210465 (EPub)

First Black Muse Publishing trade paperback edition, May 2023

Printed by Ingram Spark in the USA

www.blackmusepublishing.com

Dedication

To our amazing 3 children Autumn, Aubrey and Noah who are not only great kids but stellar students that make us proud, we dedicate this book to them for their love, sacrifices, and selflessness to share their parents with the world. You'll never come second place to the church or our careers. We love you!

Forward

"Pastor", "First Lady", "Inspirations", and now "Authors", those are just a few words that can be used to describe Nelson and Ayeisha White. Or in my case, my mom and dad. Being raised by the two, I get to see the behind-the-scenes. Has it always been glamorous and perfect as it may have seemed from the outside? No. However, it is real and laced with hard work. Not only am I a product of their love, but I have been given the amazing opportunity to watch them produce love for others. It's not just a Sunday morning thing, but rather a 24/7, 365-day occurrence. Even with energy being put into others, they still make room to choose each other.

Throughout my life, I have taken notes and looked to my parents as a guide and I hope to one day experience a love like theirs. I can confidently say that they have been a bright leading light in a world filled with darkness. Not to mention, they serve as role models when it comes to marriage and love. And yes, this book won't equate to fifteen years of learning. But it will give you insight into the wonders of a long-lasting marriage.

Autumn White

Introduction

Growing up in the projects of Southeast D.C., marriage wasn't common in my family. Not my parents, grandparents, aunties, or uncles; very few of them were married. For generations, there was no husband or wife in the home.

So, with no history of marriage in my home, I have no idea why I would propose to a young lady in middle school.

One day, I told her, "I'm going to marry you." Now what in the world would inspire a 15-year-old boy from the hood, with that background, to say and actually mean those words? But that's what happened.

I'll always remember her response. She said, "You're crazy!"

I am convinced that the church formed my consciousness around marriage. It was modeled all around me. The pastor, deacons, and youth minister all had wives, and I began to desire it for myself. I wanted to be married, too.

Fast forward to today, following the models in the church only took us so far. We were given, in general, the basics regarding marriage but needed a blueprint on how to grow and sustain a fruitful relationship. We've learned how to create a relationship and marriage that works, so we wanted to share what we've learned with you.

No matter where you are in your relationship, it's never too late to improve it!

Marriage is Under Attack

Today, more and more people believe that being married is not necessary. As far as they are concerned, its an old, obsolete tradition of the past. Statistics show that at least 40-50% of marriages will end in divorce and there is a rise among Christian couples. With these numbers, its no surprise that our faith in this institution as a society has dwindled year after year.

You'll learn in this book as long as you have a strong foundation and you have each other, you can get through any challenges or setbacks in life, but you must do the work.

It's not something you pick up when you feel like it. It's a day-by-day, month-by-month, year-by-year type of work. But, having been married for 22 years, we can attest that marriage still works if you work it.

The keyword is "work," and you must also desire it to work. Going into it thinking, "If I ever want this to be over, I'll get a divorce," is a recipe for disaster. When you realize that it's bigger than you, you'll be more inclined to take it more seriously. It all starts with a commitment to God, which is an essential message throughout this book. It's not just your partner that you're committing to, but you're also committing to God.

We hope this will be a blueprint on how to get to the altar and sustain it once you say I do.

Things are different now.

Even though we have been removed from the dating scene for over twenty-five years, being in ministry, we've seen and heard it all, and a lot has changed.

Internet dating came along and gave more liberty to single people to be whoever they wanted to be on social media. You can filter your pictures to look a certain way, bringing your best self to the light while leaving your vulnerabilities in the dark. Doing this is problematic because when you are ready to connect with someone, you don't just bring that filtered version. You have to bring your whole self to the table.

Can they handle who we really are in our dark places? We end up reserving who we are at the risk of exposing who we are. We hold back, wasting years before we can share who we are with someone else. It's hard to be vulnerable, and it takes courage to show your partner the real you. Just know good pictures develop in dark places; remember that!

Gender roles are also seemingly, a thing of the past. It used to be that the man would go out and win the bread for the family or be the provider. Women would stay home and nurture the kids and care for the home. Now we live in a day where the wives bring the bacon home, and the husbands cook it up. Even the rules of dating have changed. Now you have to safeguard yourself more than ever before. Expectations are different. I was shocked to find out that men don't pay for dates these days. In my day, it was not even a question as to who would pay. Now women are paying half, or in some cases, the whole bill. Times have truly changed.

Changing Times Requires a Change in Strategy

If the times have changed, your strategy and approach to marriage must also change. No longer can you approach marriage shooting from the hip. Instead, it would be best if you had a strategy to build a marriage and a loving family.

Now, what do I mean by "strategy"? Strategy is a plan of action or a policy designed to achieve a major goal. A strategy is the master plan, a science, or a blueprint. A strategy is a substratum or the base in which you put the plan into action to build your marriage.

Whenever a couple comes to me with plans to be married, or whenever a couple comes to me because their marriage is in trouble. I ask them these three questions.

1. *Where are you going?* The married couple should have a vision of where they see their marriage going. If they can't articulate where they are going, it's no telling where the marriage will end up. This is the first major question the couple must answer if they are going to strategically have a blueprint as it relates to the marriage. Next, there should be questions about where you see yourselves in five to ten years, like, "How many kids do we plan to have?" If you cannot answer these questions, you will have a problem with question number 2.

2. *What are you doing?* This question is a response to the first question. When you know the vision of marriage, it helps you to articulate what we are doing. The marriage has no vision if you can't answer where we are going. If there is no road map or blueprint, the couple will do whatever is right in their own

sight. However, knowing the vision of the marriage will give you clear direction. When you have clear direction, you won't do things that don't align to your destiny.

3. *How can I help you get there?* This is a major one because it speaks to how we ought to serve one another. Chick-fil-A is one of our favorite restaurants because it gives an amazing model of how service should be displayed. Chick-fil-A declares, it's my pleasure to serve you. Their number one goal when they open their doors is to serve its customers.

In a marriage, your aim and goal should always be, "How may I serve you?" When you know where you're going and when you can articulate what you are doing, there's nothing else left strategically except how can I help you get to the destination. If the husband is serving the wife and the wife is serving her husband, it's a beautiful picture of marriage working.

Finding The Right Person

What made Ayeisha the right person for me?

In my neighborhood there were very few girls that hadn't already engaged in sexual activity. When I laid eyes on Ayeisha and got to know her, I came to understand that not only was she untouched, but she was a good student. She had her sights on making marks in the world which was totally different from the girls in my neighborhood who were living in the moment. She knew there was something more to life than the here and now. At an early age, I came to realize that my destiny was attached to her.

When God revealed my purpose to me and began to show me His plan, I knew that being connected to someone was critical. As the plan for my life began to unfold, I knew Ayeisha was the right person.

You will know that you found the right one when you get a glimpse of your future and realize you cannot walk in it without attaching yourself to the one God has designated for your destiny.

Who is this book written for?

Think of this book as a marriage gumbo with enough for anyone who desires a fruitful and prosperous relationship.

Whether you're a couple that's still in the dating phase of your relationship, or you're engaged looking for the answer to that question every relationship has to answer. "Where do we go from here?"

It's even for the married couple whose relationship is flickering and needs a flame.

This book will give you direction, but also reignite the fire in couples who have been married for decades.

If you're single, this book will help you mentally prepare for the work and joys of marriage. If you don't take marriage or being in a relationship seriously, this isn't for you.

Today, dating has taken on a new meaning: you're free to date whoever you want, and see this person, that person and the person over there too. If that's you, maybe this book isn't for you. However, when you've found someone that you're ready to settle down with for potentially the rest of your life, this book will help you navigate those waters.

How to Navigate this Book

I'm realizing many people are signing up to be a husband or wife, with no idea of what it actually is. Our advice to anyone reading this book is to approach it from a place of honesty. You have to be honest with yourself, no matter what stage you're in. You'll be equipped with tools that will prepare you for marriage, but it's best received by someone who is 100% honest with themselves. Is that you?

Are you honest enough to say, I'm not a wife yet, but I believe these principles and tools will put me on the right track to becoming one. Even if you're in a marriage, you may come to realize throughout this book that maybe your spouse isn't the problem. There may be some issues in you that need to be checked. What are you bringing to the table in your marriage, and can you be honest about it?

Acknowledge where you are and know at the start is the best place to be. Churches teach that we can shout, dance, and speak in tongues, and live happily ever after. But just like in the movie Shrek (my son's favorite movie), there is no happily ever after until you once realized there was once upon a time.

Marriage is really built on that once upon a time. If you don't survive that, there will not be a happily ever after.

Why Do We Believe Marriage Still Works?

Looking at all of the obstacles of marriage, some people may say "Why should I get married?" I might as well just stay single and do me. As wonderful as that sounds, it's not about you. Establishing and maintaining any relationship can be challenging and this is especially true in a marriage. Marriage requires sacrifice and selflessness.

We value the sanction of marriage. God created us for a purpose and we believe marriage is a part of His plan for our lives.

Let's dive into the book, starting with the most important foundation that keeps your marriage working, even when things around aren't working. On this principle, everything necessary for a prosperous union is built on this.

Part I: Christ

I

Why Christ is the Foundation

While we were dating and decided to get married, we began to put down the pieces of what a marriage built on a strong foundation would look like. We knew in order to have a successful marriage, Christ who is the head of our lives, would be our foundation and through His love and guidance, we would be able to establish and build our marriage.

Undeniably, without question, building a strong foundation is impossible without the leading and the guiding of Christ. It's amazing at how many couples make a decision to be married and not model, include or welcome Christ into their marriage. In essence, it's like doing a Godly thing without God. If you desire to be married, you must first research what Christ had in mind concerning marriage. The Bible declares that one day Christ will come back for his bride which is the church. This is very interesting because Christ in this metaphor represents the husband and the church represents the bride.

If the church is the bride of Christ, it requires us as married couples to study and to learn how Christ cares, covers, collaborates, and is committed to His bride. Now, you have to understand that Christ is God in flesh so with that being said, he's hanging on the cross knowing the end of a thing before it even begins. The church will never love Him like He loves the church so now the question becomes, "How much does Christ love the church?" The answer is He died for the church. He died for us knowing that we would continue to sin, lie and cheat. Just as He demonstrated His love by giving His life, we ought to make this same sacrifice. This is a great model of true love and the foundation you must build your marriage on. Welcome Christ into your marriage. If He is not the foundation, then your marriage is on shaky ground.

We love watching HGTV's show Good Bones where they go out and look for the most horrific properties and transform them to into the most beautiful homes. Although the homes are damaged, they are built on a strong foundation. Like cement, a strong foundation keeps everything standing upright and upon it you're able to establish, build, and recreate anything. Christ is that foundation and with Him, all things are possible.

So, whether you're married, engaged, dating, or single, in order to establish a strong connection with Christ, you'll have to do some incisions inside to seal up the cracks in your foundation. You'll come out stronger and empowered to build your house, family and life on an unshakable base with good bones.

If the foundation is good, you've got everything you need to make marriage work for you. However, if the foundation is shaky and there's cracks in it, it needs to be rebuilt.

Let's dive into the importance of this foundation being in Christ.

Christ as the Foundation

Foundation is defined as an underlying base or support. With Christ as the foundation, it helps us to establish boundaries, know when we've gone too far, or when we're not doing enough. We are accountable to Him first, and this is what keeps us connected. Also, with Christ as our foundation, when tough times arise, we can stand on His word and His promises and look to Him for direction.

John 14:6 says, "I am the way, the truth and the light."

There are many beliefs and types of foundations that shape our lives, but for us, Christ has been the only way, which is THE way.

As we stated earlier, the statistics of Christian marriages that end in divorce is on the rise so tradition alone could not save us from trouble. Rather a real relationship with Christ would be the anchor that holds our marriage together. Many build their marriage on looks but looks fade away. Many build it on money but money comes and goes. Many build their marriage on their children but the kids grow old and leave the nest. When you build your marriage on Christ, it becomes the anchor that holds the marriage steady.

When we stood at the altar, in front of all our friends and family, we made our vows to love each other until death do us part. We had no idea that after having a wedding, we would have to build a marriage. A marriage is not about the wedding dress, the tuxedo, or the flowers that adorned the chapel. It wasn't even the music or doing the electric slide at the reception. It's not the pictures that will come from the photographer or the video that you will watch over and over again. That's just the wedding! What we've come to know is that many want the wedding, but few are willing to build a marriage and if marriage still works, will be your testimony, you have to be willing to get past the wedding and build a marriage. Great marriages are not wished for, they are worked on and they do not appear overnight.

Great marriages that have stood the test of time, have survived some of the most severe storms, and have passed some of life's greatest tests. If your marriage is going to work, you must indeed and in fact work at it, and the first thing you must do is lay a firm, solid foundation. Now why Christ? We realized we could not do life let alone a marriage on our own. So for us it was a no brainer. Christ had to be at the forefront of our marriage, and here is why.

Christ is our Protector

Isaiah 54:17 declares "No weapon that is formed against us shall prosper..." We often shout about the weapon and not prospering, while ignoring the fact that the weapon was formed. When you enter a marriage and decide to do life together as a married couple, there will be many weapons that will be formed against you. There will be the weapon of sickness and disease. There may be weapons of jobs being lost, families feuding or loved ones passing away. This is why we need Christ's protection. Christ is our foundation because he is our protector, and no matter what we face in life, He has a wonderful way of protecting our minds, our hearts, and our spirits to remain focused as long as we stay faithful to Him. Having Christ as a foundation does not exempt you from the trouble but it stabilizes you in it.

Christ is our Provider

In Genesis 22:14, you find Abraham at the top of the mountain getting ready to slay his son, Issac. As a matter of fact, this is the son he had been waiting for in his old age when many declared it was impossible. When Abraham lifts the knife to slay his son, God interrupts him just in the nick of time. Abraham proved his faithfulness and God spared Issac's life and He provided a ram in the bush! Because of that miracle, Abraham names the place, Jehovah Jireh, which is translated, The Lord will provide.

When you are married, and doing life together, there will be moments in your life where you will need God's supernatural provisions. There will be moments where your credit will not be enough and moments where your degree will not mean anything. There will be moments where if God does not do it, it will not get done. We are witnesses of God's supernatural provisions. We have seen Him provide over and over again in every aspect of our lives.

When we first started The House of Hope Praise Ministries, all we had was a vision and a promise from God. We started having service in a hotel with just a few of us and within 8 months, God blessed us with our current facility. We had no money and to secure the building, we had to pay the security deposit and first month's rent. God did it and nearly 8 years later, He has continued to keep our ministry.

Christ is our Promise Keeper

In Numbers 23:19, the Bible declares "God is not a man that he should lie". In other words, God is our promise keeper. If God said it, that settles it and this is a key reason why Christ is our foundation. As we matriculate through life and especially in a marriage, it is important to know that every day will not be a great day. There will be some days, where you give it your all, and still come up short. It is in these moments, your faith must rise to the occasion. If not, you will begin to take your frustration out on the ones you love. When we receive the revelation that Christ is the promise keeper, we inadvertently accept the fact that we can't do it all. So this frees us from being Superman or Superwoman, and we place the focus on the Savior; He is the great promise keeper.

Christ Keeps Us Committed

On our wedding day, we held hands and stated our vows to one another. We took this moment seriously because the commitment wasn't just to each other, it was a commitment to God.

It's also the reason why we confidently declare that divorce is not an option for us. Maybe murder but never divorce...lol.

Remember how we said it's best to approach this book with honesty?

Well, I had to be honest with myself because I knew that I could not be a leader of a wife and family if I wasn't first submitted to Christ myself.

As a husband, I had to learn how to submit my life back to the one who created it in the first place. If I was to be all that Ayeisha needed, I needed direction from a higher source who could lead me to places that I could then lead my family. And if I wanted submission from her, it would require full submission from me to Christ. Once I fully submitted to Christ, submission from her became easy.

I learned that husbands are to love their wives as Christ loved the church.

As we talked about earlier, Christ loved the church so much that He was willing to die. This is key for me to grasp because if He's asking me to love my wife the way he loved the church, what does that really mean?

In order for me to be willing to die for her, I have to be supernaturally submitted to the ultimate foundation: Christ. He will teach me how to love her because you can't produce that depth of love without first submitting to Christ.

Had my foundation not been here, and all I had was how I grew up, our marriage wouldn't have lasted.

What a Strong Foundation Looks Like

How do you transition through trouble? Can you be trusted in a trial? How do you level up during a crisis? Do you walk away, or do you work your way through it?

How you answer these questions as an individual and as a couple is the best indicator of the strength of your foundation.

The truth is, trouble is going to come. It doesn't matter who you are or where you live, in this world you will have many challenges. It's inevitable.

It may not be challenges with money; however it could be a health issue or the loss of a job. Life has a way of having ups and downs, so having a foundation for troubled times is absolutely necessary.

I remember times I could not love my wife with my money because I didn't have any. I could not love her with the testimonies of my family because there weren't any to hear.

I literally had to allow Christ to love her through me.

Many people give up in the middle of it, however, if they went back to the foundation, they would've discovered that trouble will not last. Joy comes in the morning, and this too shall pass. It may look bad right now, but there's a brighter side around the corner.

With this truth, we are empowered and given the strength we need to keep going. There were times I thought this marriage would not work, but Christ reminded me that when I was in trouble, He gave me another chance.

When I did everything through the lens and love of Christ, it made our foundation stronger. We're able to love each other, but not in our own strength. It's only through Christ that I'm able to love her, and she's able to love me.

2

How to Establish a Strong Foundation

So, how do you establish this strong foundation in your life?

The first thing you have to do is make a decision for change, and to do it from a place of honesty within yourself. Realize that what you've been doing was enough to bring you where you are today, but it will not be enough to take you where you want to go. Making a decision is tough, but you have to accept this truth.

The word "decision" is actually a medical term describing when a doctor goes in to make an incision. When making an incision, they have to cut the flesh to go inside and directly get to what the problem is.

This is why it's so tough, it requires that we're honest with what we're really dealing with, because in order to fix it, an incision will have to be made. Oftentimes, we don't want to do that.

In order to change though, we're going to have to go inside, and some areas will have to be cut. The reality is, it may not be the wife's fault that your marriage is falling apart. It may not be the kids that are making it challenging. It could very well be you.

When establishing and building this foundation, you have to give God your whole heart. This is the kind of work that starts from within yourself. From here, He can begin to heal and deal with you from the inside out. It will start slow, but soon, you'll find it working it's way on the outside.

It is imperative to be fully submitted to Christ, because you will need something solid to stand on in troubled times. Especially in the times when you realize everything you've done up until this point, may not get you to the next stage in your life journey.

How Strong is Your Foundation?

Your foundation is the glue, the anchor or base that is holding the structure or in this case the marriage up.

If the foundation is not solid and sure, your marriage is built on shaky ground. You will know how solid your foundation is when tough times come!

Anybody can testify that their marriage is great when things are going great but when the marriage is tested, the foundation it's built on will speak!

I remember a tough time in our marriage when my wife's father died and my wife came to me and asked me would I move out of my new home that we had just purchased to make sure her mom, who is now a widow would be ok.

It was a huge test because we had struggled and saved for this home. We had been through disappointment and discouragement and now God had blessed us with this home and now my wife is asking me to move so her mom would be comfortable in this next season.

In my flesh I was saying hell no but my foundation which is Christ told me if you have the strength to sacrifice, I have the power to bless you.

I had to put my flesh aside and allow Christ to manifest and it was at that point we begin to water the foundation of our marriage.

How strong is your foundation? Can it stand to be tested? Can it survive the storms life can bring simply by living? If not, make a declaration to begin to water the roots of your foundation and watch God blossom your marriage into an amazing flower.

Christ Creates Order in The Home

When our family began to grow, I struggled as a mother and often put our kids before my husband. My focus was on the kids, and I forgot like most Christian couples that there's a model for marriage.

The model is God, husband, wife and then children. For the first 7 years of our marriage, it was just the two of us so things were good. However, when our family began to expand, my focus immediately shifted towards the children. Before you judge me, let me explain. We lost our first child, which really took a toll on me emotionally so when God finally blessed us with children, I went into Super Mommy mode. After all my husband was a strong man. Our children were helpless and defenseless and if anyone was going to protect them it would be me right?

I gave motherhood all I had and when it came to the marriage, I found myself depleted and empty. I was tired, weary and I began to shift the blame on my husband. After all, I carried his children for 9 months and my body went through all kind of changes. I was up late at night while he slept so he should understand why there is no sex tonight or why there is no date night.

As a consequence, my marriage was suffering. It was like a bank account where you make withdrawals but never make any deposits and you're left with insufficient funds.

On the other hand, I just knew I was mother of the year. Can you see the dichotomy? Mother of the year but what about being a wife?

I prayed and God begin to speak to me and declare order in the house. He also revealed to me that my children will one day grow old and leave the nest and start a family of their own. Was I setting a good example of the model for marriage? Nope!

If your connection to your spouse is only through your children, your marriage is disconnected. I realized that I'm a wife first and it was time for me to step up. Plus, my husband was sick of me. LoL.

It's important to create order in your home, especially in our roles as husband and wife. I had to respect my husband's role as the provider and recognize my role as the receiver.

I began to ask God to show me areas in me that were out of balance and I realized that not only was I neglecting my husband but I was neglecting myself as well. If I don't take care of me, I'm no good to anyone so I took time to invest in myself with some much needed self care. I pampered myself with relaxing baths, reading books and quiet walks.

When God showed me, with his guidance and grace, I was able to find the balance that I needed to maintain a happy home. Once I got myself together, everything fell into place. I was in a better place to give my husband what he needed and surprisingly my husband began to find ways he could bless me. He helped out more by cooking meals and running my bath water. The bible is true when you give, God will give it back in good measure.

I encourage you to make an investment of time and energy in each other first. Date night at least twice a month is a must for us. Your children do not come first. Don't make the mistake of giving your all to the children, and leftovers to each other. When the kids grow up leave home, what will you have left if you never continued growing together as one? The last thing you want to do is look up and realize you've been sleeping with a stranger for years!

Part II: Commitment

2

What is Commitment?

Commitment by definition is an engagement or an obligation that restricts freedom of action.

Now let's unpack this. To be married requires commitment which by definition restricts you from being free to do what you want, how you want, whenever you want to do it. I don't believe you can do whatever you want and still consider yourself committed.

When we speak of someone who is uncommitted in a marriage, we automatically jump to infidelity. But you can be uncommitted in your mind long before you enter someone else's arms. As a matter of fact, it starts in the mind and flows to the body. So if the breakdown to an uncommitted marriage starts in the mind, the buildup to a committed marriage also starts in the mind.

As you read this chapter, ask yourself as it relates to your marriage, what's on your mind? The Bible says as a man or woman thinks in his heart, so is he. If your thoughts are not to build up your marriage, you could be having thoughts to tear it down. Examine your thoughts and ask God to take what you think about your marriage to another level. As you think higher, your marriage will soar higher! A committed marriage is a winning marriage and if you can stay committed, you can get through anything together.

When we speak of someone who is committed, it is to suggest they are present and accountable and dependable. Commitment ties back to Christ, our foundation. When your marriage is built on a solid and sure foundation, you understand that your foundation has been built on someone who is committed to you. This is major and very important because it requires each individual to approach the marriage with honesty.

When we look back over our lives, and we consider the mistakes we've made and the moments where we didn't dot every "I" or cross every "T". Or the moments where we disappointed Christ over and over again and yet his love for us never changed and He remained consistent and committed to us. When you view commitment through this lens, you are not so easily to give up or throw in the towel when things are not conducive in your own marriage. Your mind should reflect back and take an inventory over your life when Christ, who is the foundation of your marriage, was committed to you when you were acting unlovable.

Three Requirements for Commitment

Discipline

Many people suggest practice makes perfect. I disagree. I believe that perfect practice makes perfect. Discipline is an order or strictness for a regiment in which one practices over and over. When you consider the word commitment, it will require discipline. Now it's really easy to suggest you're committed when you don't have options; however, when you can pick, choose and refuse, the question becomes, how committed are you? It seems like every married couple I talk to these days have the same testimony.

No one was asking for my number before I got married but as soon as I began to walk around with my wedding ring on, it seems like the wedding ring made me all the more attractive. The truth of the matter is no one wants what no one wants. It's not until you get with someone that everyone wants you. This is where you have to be disciplined. You have to say no, stay no and remain true to whom you are committed to.

Many marriages start out committed; however, they don't stay committed. It requires discipline to say no because the truth of the matter is, every day will not be a good day. You have to discipline your flesh so that you don't lose your favor.

Determination

Determination deals with your willpower, your inner strength, and your focus. When you are in a committed relationship, you must be absolutely determined to let nothing separate you from your spouse. There will be moments, times, and people to come along and test your discipline and your determination. What we have discovered in 22 years of marriage is misery loves company. The enemy does not come after marriages already in trouble, rather the enemy comes to bust marriages that are making moves and taking steps. When you are in a marriage that is working together in harmony, make no mistake about it, the enemy is coming to test the strength of the marriage. You must be determined in your resolve and your willpower, so that your commitment remains intact.

Dedication

When you are dedicated, your heart is in it. You have a zeal and a tenacity and your allegiance to your partner speaks for itself. You don't have to convince others you're committed because your dedication speaks to the commitment.

When you are dedicated, you don't view it as a struggle or a sacrifice. It speaks to the service, honor, and privilege you have to share and do life with your partner. Dedication does not come overnight, rather you become dedicated when you are disciplined in your commitment, and you are determined not to let anything, or anyone ruin that commitment.

How to Commit and Stay Committed

Here's the secret to commitment: Christ. It's through Him that we strengthen our commitment one to another and understand that we can't just do whatever we want.

If Christ is not pleased, it's also going to disrupt the relationship that we have in the physical. If it's not strong in the spiritual, it's not going to work in the natural.

Oftentimes couples will highlight the natural and overlook the spiritual. Some couples only marry for money and sex. They aren't necessarily in love, but they love what money has afforded them like a nice home or a luxury car. When you marry for money only, it's not destiny, it's dangerous.

Here's the truth: Money will come if you marry the right person, and for the right reasons. The right person will push you into your purpose. When you are walking in your purpose, prosperity will follow. When you view marriage as ministry, money will come.

Let's talk about sex! Sex should be enjoyed in the parameters of marriage. However, sex cannot be the totality of the marriage. For some, the sex is so good, it's not about loving the other person. It's about an emotional connection to what they get in the bedroom. There's no meaningful connection or good communication. Sex cannot be the weight in which the marriage is standing. When you marry the right person and walk in your purpose, your sex life will go to another level.

We were in our early 20s, and didn't have any money, nor did we know what an orgasm was. It wasn't about the sex or money for us either. Rather the person and the purpose. The closer we got to purpose, the more explosive our sex life became!

Once we made sex secondary to the Savior, our commitment to one another became stronger.

How do we do that? We find ourselves in Worship and the Word. From this we draw the strength and wisdom that helps us produce a winning marriage.

It's simple. If my foundation is off-balance, so will my commitment be to my spouse.

So, to commit and stay committed, we commit to worship. When we go to worship, it's not just a religious routine. We're in worship, and the word takes root in our marriage. We hear the word and apply it to our lives.

One of the commandments that speaks seriously to this says, "Thou shall have no other God before me."

Once I dishonor my commitment by bringing someone else into the relationship, the whole structure of my marriage is compromised. Be careful to not put anyone or anything before this commitment to Christ, and to your spouse.

Many people are going to church without any expectation to have an encounter with God. They're going to worship because their grandparents went to church, or because their wife asked them to go because she senses something is off in their marriage. Simply going to church isn't going to fix these challenges.

The Word and the Worship have to actually be applied in order to take root in your life. In other words, if nothing changes, nothing will change. It's through intimate worship and washing yourself with the Word that we strengthen our connection.

Make A Choice

To commit will require you to make a Choice and to stick with it. Many start out strong in their marriage, but they don't stay strong, and they don't finish strong. Commitment means I say yes and stay yes!

It's easy to say yes when the times are good, but can you stay yes when the times get tough? Life will test your yes! The devil hates marriage. The Bible says he comes to steal, kill, and destroy. His main objective is to turn your yes into divorce. Should your marriage end in divorce, you will soon find out it was easy to enter but difficult to exit. Now you must deal with the chaos of deciding what to do with the house, the kids, and the money. That can be chaotic!

So how do we stay committed when we have outside forces working overtime to turn our commitment into chaos?

It goes back to what we said earlier. We need the help of Christ. Christ is the anchor that cements our commitment. He is the anchor our marriage grips when times get tough. The Bible's says, "When the enemy rushes in like a flood He will lift up a standard against him". Our commitment to him will anchor our commitment to each other!

3

The Root of Infidelity

Why do people cheat? Why do they go outside of their commitment and function as a single person when they know they are married? It all falls back to where our foundation lies in the beginning. If there is no commitment to Christ, you won't have a true commitment to anyone else.

Oftentimes, a person who cheats on their spouse is trying to fulfill a desire or void that really can't be filled by another person. Sex at its core was not designed for your enjoyment only, there is a purpose behind it. To have intercourse and be intimate means allowing someone else to see-into-me. That's what intimacy is.

It's much deeper than just the physical, so if I'm going to break the commitment and run the risk of losing it, I must ask myself the question, what is this really about?

It's crazy to have intercourse with someone you have not made a commitment to. Some people hide how much money they have in the bank but will freely sleep with someone else. Your body is a temple, and it's one of the most precious gifts that you have. To give it away to someone you don't even know or are not committed to, speaks to the void on the inside that can only be filled by Christ.

When people say they cheated, it was because they say they weren't getting what they wanted in the relationship. The truth be told, there may be something off in the marriage, but many couples realize when it comes to intimacy, they'd been disconnected long before they stopped sleeping with each other. The connection got off track.

If this is you, I advise you to examine the motives as to why you got married in the first place.

Remember to be married means to be entangled with another person, which means it's not about you only anymore. Commitment at its core means we're tied together, and selfishness must go on the back burner.

So, let's get to the root of the matter! Many think infidelity starts with intercourse with someone who is not your spouse but intercourse is the result not the root. The Root is the seed that has been planted in the head long before you ever reach the bed. The enemy is not after your bed as much as he wants to get into your head!

Joyce Meyer says in her book, Battlefield of the Mind, that "the battle is won or lost in our mind." The Bible declares "Be transformed by the renewing of your mind." It also talks about adopting the mindset of Christ. "Let this mind be in you, which is also in Christ Jesus."

If the devil plants seeds of doubt, seeds of lust, or seeds of the grass being greener on the other side, those seeds will plant itself in your mind and soon it will produce a bed of infidelity.

So, we have to renew our mind about our marriage daily. We must adopt the mindset of Christ, speak the marriage we want to see and plant seeds of love, honor, hope, faithfulness, and desire. When those kinds of seeds are planted, the roots of infidelity are strangled, and the devil is defeated.

How Do We Water Our Roots?

We water our roots through worship and the word. When it comes to marriage, there will be good days and bad days but no more single days. When you are single, you have a choice to stay but when you are married, you are committed to see it through. When we water our roots of marriage, we take the good with the bad and believe that the best is yet to come!

When we worship God, He changes our perspective. My spouse may not be what I want them to be yet but one-day I will see what God said.

The word seals it. The closer you get to God through His word; it reveals who you are rather than who your spouse is not. When you see your own shortcomings, you are less likely to hold your spouse to a standard you yourself are not meeting when it comes to God.

Pay Attention to Each Other

It's essential to pay attention to each other. With my wife, I need to know what kind of mood she's in, and what turns her on. What got her going in year 10 may not be what's doing it for her in year 20.

What I do know is that I'm committed enough to keep the fire burning. I have to be able to look beyond what I want and consider what my wife needs.

Tips To Help You Pay Attention

1. Listen

   You must listen to your spouse versus just hearing them. Your spouse is communicating when he or she is speaking and when they are not. If you don't move from hearing to listening, you will miss what is actually being communicated.

   Hearing is found on the surface. Listening connects you on a deeper level and moves you past the surface and into the heart and the mind of your spouse. It puts you in tune with the tone of voice, the movement of the body language and the rhythm of the conversation.

2. Respond

   To respond is to reply. There is nothing worse than sharing your life with someone that does not have the capacity to respond. If I share my heart with you and tell you how I feel, the worst thing you can do is ignore, dismiss, or disregard them. It's really a sign of disrespect and once a spouse feels disregarded or disrespected, you are in the danger zone.

3. Adjust

   To make an adjustment means I've listened to you, I responded to you and now I'm taking it in and making an adjustment. I remember early on in our marriage my wife would fuss about me leaving my clothes everywhere. I didn't think it was a big deal because I was hearing and not listening. Not listening to her was a sign of disregard and disrespect and I was in the danger zone of having dirty clothes lol. So I decided to listen, respond and make an adjustment. Now I enjoy having clean clothes because I place them where they are supposed to be and not all over the house.

I encourage you to pay more attention to your spouse and watch the relationship soar.

How May I Serve You? Serving Your Spouse Strengthens the Commitment

Christ had a mind to serve, and to endure suffering. We are not lowering ourselves when we're serving our spouse. Rather, because we are confident and committed in who we are, we don't mind serving each other.

When my father-in-law passed, we had to endure some challenging moments, and as a husband, I had to adopt the mind of Christ to be what my wife and family needed me to be. I had to rearrange my vision of what our marriage was, and question, can I love her enough to be committed while we help navigate her mother through this life-turn?

My life does not belong to me. I had to serve and endure suffering for that season, and it's only possible through Christ. Adopting a mindset of Christ is necessary in marriage to serve and submit to one another, even when times are hard.

You may ask why is God allowing us to go through this in this season? This storm, this trouble that has landed on our doorstep may not even be for us, but we have to endure it because there are other couples looking at how we're navigating this, and it may give them hope to know that hardship are lessons that we don't understand at the present moment but it's all happening for a reason.

We've Cheated!

Okay before you have a heart attack, no we didn't physically cheat. We didn't fall into the arms of another person, nor did we end up in someone else's bed. As a matter of fact, many people have reduced cheating to having sex with another person, but I submit to you that's not the only form of cheating. When you have devoted yourself to someone or something and give it more attention than your spouse, that's cheating.

One of the definitions of cheating is to avoid or to break promises. To not remain true to your word is cheating. As we take inventory over the past 22 years, we regret to inform you that yes, we have cheated.

When the kids were born my wife engulfed herself and gave herself over to motherhood and that's cheating.

When I became a Pastor, I fell in love with the church and devoted myself to doing the work of the ministry and oftentimes my wife and my family suffered because I put the needs of the church first. That's cheating! My wife and I missed out on date nights and spending quality alone time with one another, and it really took a toll on our marriage. I had become so consumed with being the perfect pastor and building the kingdom, that I left my home and relationship unguarded.

Anything that is causing an imbalance can be summed up as cheating. Anything that's causing your spouse to feel neglected, disregarded, unimportant, or unappreciated are forms of cheating.

Our prayer for you is now you have the tools to strengthen your commitment to God, which will in turn strengthen your commitment to your spouse.

Part III: Communication

4

Communication

In this section, you'll learn how whenever the enemy attacks a marriage, his number one weapon is to get the husband and wife to stop talking.

Just like the breakdown in the garden of Eden? It was a lack of communication!

Eve wasn't communicating with Adam. Instead, she was talking with the serpent, and he got her to eat the fruit off the tree. When God gave the instructions on what they could and could not do, he gave it to Adam, which represents the husband in this construct. He tells Adam you can enjoy this and that, but this tree you cannot touch.

Adam was now supposed to go and share those instructions with his wife, so she now is in line with what God required. However, because he failed to communicate, everything got damaged! The power of life and death indeed is in your mouth.

When troubles arise, the lack of effective communication (which includes speaking and listening) is the main cause of breakdown in the marriage. Think about it: If I'm not talking to my spouse, who am I talking to?

It's essential to communicate because it produces power and possibility in what the marriage can be. Without this, we're living in the cemetery of what's about to die. When the silence starts up, so does the chaos.

This section on communication will help you move out of the dead place and into the possibility of what can be accomplished when you know the power of your words.

5

The Cause of Breakdown in Communication

Our words can produce life and death; they are that powerful. Most of us just don't understand how powerful our words are, especially in marriage.

Through communication, we learn how to navigate through the tribulation and find the lesson we're supposed to take from it, knowing that it will pass. However, if we shut down, the relationship is in trouble. Communication will produce life in the marriage so keep it strong against any circumstance.

The root of communication breakdowns are brought about by the issues of life that tend to invade marriages. When we talk about life, the stress of a job, the arrival of children, the trouble kids are navigating in school, drama with the extended family, they can all attack your communication like you wouldn't believe.

It all comes from the external, and if communication lines go down between you two, you're dismissing one of the saving graces that marriage brings about in life. Just by talking, you'll grow the marriage muscles needed to face life together. You'll learn to appreciate these challenges, because they bring you closer to God and to each other. However, if you're disconnected from worship and the word, the same challenges can push you away from each other.

Our Breakdown

As we talked about earlier, one of the most challenging times in our marriage came when we first became parents.

We were not speaking, nor were we on one accord. We couldn't figure it out for some time, but we realized my wife was focused on being a mother first and put being a wife to the back burner. This is common in many marriages, but the lesson learned is that your relationship with each other comes first, then the kids. We both had to learn our roles through this tough time.

When there is a breakdown in the communication, three things must happen:

1. Recognize that there is an issue.
   One of the worst things a couple can do is pretend there is no issue when there clearly is an issue. In alcohol anonymous class, one of the first things they tell you is to admit there is a problem. You can't address what you're not willing to admit and you will never conquer what you refuse to face! You have to face the truth and come together and admit there is a problem.
2. Fight to restore the connection.
   I live in the house with 3 kids who are constantly on the

internet and a wife who works from home. Whenever the WiFi is down, there is a fight to restore the connection! We check every box, we check the electricity, we call the provider, and we don't rest until we have solved the problem. With that same energy and that same determination, we must fight to restore the connection in our relationships. The enemy knows there is power in words, so he wants to keep you silent! You have to fight to restore the communication, and sometimes the best way is to over communicate. Talk about everything.

3. Identify when it happened and what caused it so you don't repeat the same cycle.

    If you never get down to what caused the issue, you can never repair it. Many will suggest, let's not talk about it and sweep it under the rug, but the issue will resurface. Since we have moved into our home, I love doing yard work and planting flowers. Every now and then a weed will rise to the surface. Often, in the same spot that it was removed from before. You have to get down to the root of the issue, so we don't repeat it again!

Once we acknowledged the breakdown in communication, we realized that the other comes first, and that's when things began to turn around and get better.

Speaking Two Different Languages

Have you ever heard the phrase men are from Mars women are from Venus? This typically means that men and women don't naturally speak the same language. When it comes to communication, this is in fact true. In order to build up communication in your marriage, you have to learn each other's love language, which is both verbal and non-verbal.

Everything is a conversation. From your body language and facial expressions to the amount of time it takes to respond to a text message or email. Even the way you look at each other is a form of communication.

Communication is the medium in which we send and receive information. It is the heartbeat in which the marriage has a rhythm and flow. Where there is no communication, there will be stagnation that could possibly lead to separation or ultimately devastation. Communication also eliminates confusion, and it is very hard to be confused about something you've communicated about.

Tevin Campbell had a song entitled, "Can We Talk". Talking is where you learn about one another. I can't tell you how many married couples I have counseled down throughout the years only to discover they leaped in marriage without first learning the person. A lot of chaos and confusion could have been avoided, if only we had learned before we leaped!

Learning through Communication

It is through communication and learning one another, we discover how you were raised, what's your value system, do you believe in God, what's your credit score, do you have a savings account and a 401(k) plan? These are very important questions that definitely have to be communicated when you are in a relationship. It is in the learning process, where you discover the likes and dislikes and the strengths and weaknesses. The more we know about one another, the more you know how to love each other.

Loving through Communication

Teach me how to love you. Many people ascribe to the theory, love at first sight. It's possible however, we see it a different way, lust at first sight. Love is a learning process. If you hardly communicate and learn one another, you can never fully love one another. It's through the learning process, you make a decision to love someone. Anyone can love the strong you, however the more I learn about your weaknesses, I have a decision to make. Do I proceed with what I have learned, or do I hit the pause button because this is too much!

Being married for 22 years, we have definitely learned one another and we are in fact still learning one another. I am not the most neat and organized person. My wife, on the other hand is very neat and organized. She eats in a very particular kind of way and I have learned how to order her food. I've come from a single parent home and she grew up in a two parent home, so we had to learn each other's value systems. We have learned to love one another and now we can live on another level.

Living through Communication

Communication is a very powerful tool for married couples. When you communicate well, you can live on a different level. Communication reveals the details of the marriage. We love this new age technology where we can text and email, however; there is nothing like old fashion conversation. It is through conversation; we understand the tone and we learn the value of listening. Oprah Winfrey said, "Love is in the details" Your communication should be so strong that you look beyond the surface and go deep into the details of the relationship. This is very critical because details keep you from danger and danger keeps the marriage from derailing.

When you communicate to your spouse, it's up to them to take what you've said, compartmentalize it, and make the adjustments as necessary. If you're on the receiving end, you can't just dismiss what they've shared. It's best to internalize it and just see it for what it is. You may not be happy about it at the moment but put yourself in your spouse's shoes and picture how you would feel.

To not do this results in one of you saying, "You're just not getting what I'm saying!" And if the same issue keeps coming up, and an adjustment hasn't been made, it's going to produce all kinds of frustration. Sometimes our wires get crossed when we're saying one thing, and it's being interpreted to mean something completely different. This is why it's important to be intentional and mean what you say.

In a marriage, it is super important to speak the same language. As we mentioned earlier and as the Bible teaches us, there is power in words. There is a power, a synergy, and a rhythm when you speak the same language. When you speak the same language, it's a sign that the marriage is operating in unity and you are on one accord.

Communication Produces Fruit

Circling back to our foundation, the closer we grow to Christ, the more He shows us who we really are. With this, it's revealed that we are one, and what it is that your spouse may need!

Jesus said, "I am the vine. You are the branches. If you abide in me and I in you, then together we can bear much fruit, but apart from me, you can do nothing."

The more we communicate our needs, the more we begin to speak with each other, and the power of being on one accord will start to produce fruit. However, the more we stay silent and never try to understand each other, the disconnection will produce chaos.

The Ultimate Communication: Prayer

Get a picture of the cross in your mind, it's a powerful and unforgettable symbol. You'll see there's a vertical and horizontal line that makes that cross, which symbolizes the importance of balance in our personal and spiritual relationship.

Our spiritual relationship with God is represented by the vertical line and the horizontal line represents our relationship to each other physically. What's beautiful about this symbolism is that God will never intrude himself in a physical connection, because He's spiritual and has to be invited. In other words, God is not going to be a wife to me, and He's not going to be a husband to my wife. However, He instructs and teaches me how to be my best.

When tough times arise, it's essential to stay in communication with God through prayer so we can hear from Him. In fact, it's the most important communication in your relationship. Prayer is the ultimate communication because it brings everything back into alignment, no matter the circumstance. Being in alignment with God through prayer also gives you insight into what your spouse needs most, even when they don't have the words. How powerful!

6

The Best Tips for
Communication

It's really key to listen and internalize what's being communicated versus being quick to respond. Here are some words of wisdom that will help you communicate in a way that's effective and productive in your relationship.

Don't Be Defensive

We are often more quick to defend our position on a matter, than we are to develop purpose in an important conversation. It's so bad sometimes, that the other person can be saying something and the only thing on your mind is on what you're going to say next.

If you want to develop purposeful communication, listen to the actual problem first, and don't be defensive. 90% of the time it may not even be about you! Your spouse just needs to be able to share what's on their mind or heart and be heard. If we establish a mind to listen and put down the defenses, we'll find ourselves closer and able to actually hear each other.

Admit When You're Wrong

I told my wife I didn't want our kids to have cell phones and be exposed to the internet too soon. She insisted that they should have a phone in case we needed to reach them. I thought because we usually pick them up after school, what emergency would require them to have a phone?

My wife later admitted that she was wrong to go with that decision. She doesn't like that they're on their phone so much now and can't imagine what they're seeing on the internet. Thankfully there are safety measures in place for our children today, but this is a situation where honest communication, and admitting when you're wrong gives a deeper meaning to what it means to be a purposeful communicator. Seek to develop the conversation by resisting the need to be defensive and admit when you're wrong. It says a lot about you to do that.

Be Open

It's important to develop the skill of creating an environment where open communication is always appropriate and welcome.

The best way to do that is to have an open-door policy in your relationship. There should never be a time while building a life with another person, that they feel like they can't come talk to you.

They could very well see something you can't see, or bring insight you don't have. Move from crawling to walking by coming together in agreement in your communication and keep the lines open at all times.

R&R: The Keys to Communication in Marriage

We're not talking about rest and relaxation. This is a new R&R. The key to communication in a relationship is respect and reverence.

If you're not able to respect and revere your spouse for who they are, you won't include them in your conversations, and they won't include you. If these are not established in your communication, it'll be easy to put another person and consider them and their opinion higher than the one you said, "I do."

You wouldn't have a problem talking with or respecting the opinion of a millionaire or someone of a higher status, but you do with the person you sleep with every night? Without respect and reverence, you're at risk of making life decisions alone and the trust in the relationship going down the drain.

There has to be a common respect for each other, where you value what the other brings to the table. There also has to be a reverence for the other person, and a mindset that says to the other, "I honor you and what you have to say." "I respect your opinion, and there's nothing I don't value about you or what you have to say. I respect you enough to include you in this conversation." This means that you hold your spouse in high esteem and want them at the table with you.

Part IV: Covering

7

Covering

What is Covering?

Webster defines the word covering as to guard, to protect, to fight for, to maintain and to shield from present and future attacks. To cover someone really says, "When you are not at your best, I still got you."

Christ is our ultimate covering, and it's not contingent on our behavior or even the mistakes we make.

Jesus said, "I'll never leave you nor forsake you." There's nothing you can do to make me stop loving you. I won't even remember your sins and shortcomings. I'll put them in the sea of forgetfulness. I won't bring it up again. This is what Christ says to us, and that's why He's our ultimate covering, always willing to restore us and create within us a new heart and renew a right spirit.

It's through Christ that we are able to forgive, because He forgave us and it's through Him that we can love even when we are unlovable because that's how He loves us. Through Christ's love, we are able to give each other another chance because Christ has given us chance after chance more than we can count.

If God can cover us, why can't we cover our spouse?

When entering a marriage, the Bible is clear in Mark 10:8 which states "and the two shall become one flesh." When you become one, what impacts one person will impact the whole marriage. So, if what impacts you, affects me, it will be to our benefit to cover one another. Now to suggest that we need to cover one another is to also suggest there will be attacks and storms that will come our way.

These are things we don't consider as we are standing up at the altar on our wedding day but the truth of the matter is, life happens to all of us and it's a lot easier knowing your partner has you covered.

Many don't realize marriage is a connection like no other. When you say I do, you're not only connecting spiritually and physically but you're also connecting governmentally.

One of the mistakes many make is they agree with their mouth to be married but everything about their movements suggest they are still single.

When you are married, whatever your partner is dealing with has attached itself to you. So if they are going through spiritual warfare, you both are going through spiritual warfare. If they are suffering with health issues, you may not be hurting or have a bad diagnosis but guess what? You have now become the chief doctor and or the head nurse.

If your spouse is bad with money, or has accumulated a mountain of debt, a pile of parking tickets, or is behind on his or her child support, it has now landed on your doorstep. The best way to stay Connected while you're battling life's Critical moments is to Cover one another. To know someone is covering you and has your back is one of the greatest experiences in being married. You're reassured through them that everything is going to be alright and that your foundation is secure.

We Are Each Other's Biggest Supporters

In marriage, after God's protection, we have to be the first line of defense for each other.

It's important that before anyone else, you are each other's biggest cheerleader. No one's voice should be louder than your spouse. The power of life and death is in the tongue. In order to properly cover your spouse, it's key to know that it all starts in your mind first and then makes its way to your mouth.

After I preach, I always ask my wife "How was the sermon? How did I do?" Her response is always, "Babe, it was awesome!"

I know that I'm not always at my best each and every time, but I figured out that she says this because we all are the most vulnerable when we're operating in our gifts and purpose. We often gravitate towards the applause, and away from the aggravation.

Whether it's a church sermon or a presentation at work, afterwards we're each the most vulnerable and in need of validation. Our spirit becomes empty from pouring out passions, and even though we're physically tired, we are still drawn to the applause.

If my wife gets her hair done, and I don't say anything about it, that's going to be a problem. If Jim at work says "Oh, Ayeisha, that's a nice color on you," she will naturally gravitate towards that applause and pull away from the agitation of not being acknowledged by her spouse.

On the contrary, if negative energy is present from another person, especially my spouse, I'm inclined to move away from it and towards where I'm being acknowledged. That's natural. We like what we like, and acknowledgement and applause feels good. However, if the one you're connected to cannot do that, you and the relationship may be in trouble.

It may not be the best time to be critical and ask, "Why didn't you say that?" or "I didn't really agree with what you said or did." Again, timing is everything and there's a time and place for criticism and feedback. If the outside applause is going to be alluring, the home cannot be aggravating. It has to be a place of covering and restoration.

Galatians 6:1 says, "Brother, if any man or woman be overtaken, you which is more spiritual restore such a one in the spirit of meekness, considering yourself lest you also fall."

A true testament of your spirituality lies in your ability to cover and restore your partner when they have fallen short. Until they are in the place to be the husband or wife you know them to be, commit to covering them.

There will be times in your marriage when you don't hit every mark. If one of you fall short, the one who is "more spiritual" can bring about restoration in the other.

Three Areas of Covering

There are 3 areas you will have to cover your spouse that will be critical in your marriage.

1. The Past

   All of us have made some mistakes in the past and all of us have done some things in the past we are not proud of. We all have something in the past that we wish we could erase and undo but no matter how much you try to bury it, forget it, or ignore it, you can't escape it. So, when the past rears its ugly head, the worst thing your spouse needs to feel is that he or she is in this alone.

   I can't tell you how many couples I have counseled, and they have suggested this is their spouse's problem and not my problem or they say this was before me and this does not concern me.

   I remember when we first got married there were some bad decisions, I made concerning my credit. I signed for some things and committed my name to some loans when I was single that impacted my life as a married man.

   I was single, driving reckless and mounted many tickets which in turn produced a bad driving record. Well, it didn't impact anyone but me; however, when I got married, my driving record became attached to my wife's perfect record which in turn made our insurance bill super high.

   My wife had every reason to be upset and to be angry, but the truth of the matter is she chose to fall in love and to marry someone who had made bad credit choices and had a bad driving record. Do you have the stamina to cover someone who have made mistakes in their past?

   These are examples of mistakes made in the past regarding the history of bad decisions and money management but what about the childhood trauma caused by mental or physical abuse or what if your spouse never got past the divorce of their parents? Do you have the stamina to cover that? These are really important questions that definitely need to be addressed if you want to maintain a healthy marriage.

2. The Present

The present is in this moment. It's the here and the now. We are living in a day where the job market is crazy and when you said I do, you had no idea you may have to cover your spouse financially because of a job that no longer exists. What about the spouse who wakes up in the morning and because of the state of the economy, their 401k has been wiped out. This is critical because if you're not on one accord, finances can cause major issues in marriages.

When our kids were young, we were spending an enormous amount of money in childcare. We both had good paying jobs, but the cost of childcare was consuming most of our earnings. We were behind in our bills, and it caused a lot of strain and stress in our marriage. So, my wife and I made the decision for me to quit my job and start my own childcare business. That way I would be able to take care of my own kids while still providing for my family. There were periods where I had no income coming in, so this took a lot of patience from the both of us. We were able to make it through this tough time, but it taught us the importance of covering one another.

3. Physically

You may also need to cover your spouse physically. Have you thought about what happens if your partner gets in an accident, or your partner suffers sickness and is unable to move around and to do things they use to do? Have you considered how your spouse would respond to the loss of a mother, father, grandmother or a friend and what their mental state would be? How will they bounce back and how long will it take for them to recover?

What happens if your partner does the unthinkable, the unimaginable and fall in the arms of another? Not only that but the news is getting out about it all around the town and all over the internet. To everyone else it's just speculation but you are the only one who can bring validation to the rumors that are circulating in the air.

What will you do and how will you handle it because it's really not credible until you make a decision to cover or not to cover.

Before you decide, there are three things to remember:

1. Grace Given and Grace Received
   We have all needed grace and will one day need it again. Remember, what you sow is what you will reap. Many will seek after grace when they are in trouble or going through trials and tribulations. They feel that when they are going through, the world must stop what they are doing and snatch them out at all costs. People are good at seeking grace when they are in need, but bad at serving it to someone else when they are in need. Sow grace in their trouble and be served grace in your trouble.

2. Value Your Vows
   The Bible says it's better to not make a vow at all than to make one and break it.
   A vow is defined as an oath, a pledge, a promise, a commitment. After the dress and the suit are hung up, after the makeup is off and the line dances have come to an end, the married couple must now make and cultivate a life of their

own. When storms and devastation hit, they must remind themselves of the vows they made to each other. For better and for worse, in sickness and in health. To love and be committed no matter what.

3. The Mission/Marriage is not Impossible

Rest in the fact that God loved you so much so that he has placed this awesome assignment into your hands to cover your spouse. People will say you are crazy and some will suggest what they would do if they were in your shoes; however, they are not and they don't have your assignment. Tupac had a song entitled "It's me against the world" When you become one it really is you two against the world. The bible says let a man leave his mother and father and cleave to his wife. To cleave means to draw close to or to forsake others and to grab hold of your spouse.

When you cleave and cover, you understand that to cover them means to protect you.

Cover in the good times and cover in the bad times and when you do it, God will trade your covering seasons for a season of celebration that will be proportional to the way you covered!

8

Limits

Are There Limits?

So, we just explained why you should cover. But let's talk about the limits to the covering. Is there a limit? When do I say enough is enough? When do I reach my covering capacity?

When times get rough and you are not sure when it's enough, God will show you when this is no longer a marriage or partnership.

Limits and boundaries are a necessity to a fruitful partnership. Even in a marriage, you have to put some healthy limits and boundaries in place and communicate them clearly.

Four Limits of Covering

When Covering You is Crippling Me

Notice I didn't say hurting me, devastating me, or embarrassing me. All of these things are major and leave a nasty taste in your mouth, but we use the word crippling. Crippling is defined as severe and disabling damage and it deprives you of the ability to function normally. When I'm loving you and losing myself we now have a bigger problem.

Here is a sign of when Covering becomes Crippling

When Your Core value has been Compromised
There used to be some things that were non-negotiable and some things we would never do. There used to be some things that we would hear and immediately dismiss. Now you find yourself Compromising on the Core value that have made you who you are today.

When Your Decision-Making is Destructive
You used to be able to call right, "right" and call wrong, "wrong". You used to be able to make a clear and sound decision. Now your decision making has now progressed from being clear to chaotic. Now your bad choice to cover someone who refuses to change is so chaotic it's crippling the entire family.

Your Destiny has become Distant
You and your spouse used to have goals, and plans. You used to have aspirations and dreams. What happened to the vacation home plans? What happened to the college fund for the kids? What happened to the retirement fund and the LLC that you were going to do? Of course, life happens, and obstacles will come but if your goals are slipping further and further away due to meaningless excuses, you may want do a re-evaluation.

As I Cover You , You're Not Covering Me

Have you ever asked yourself, why am I doing all the giving and they are doing all the taking? Or in this case, why am I constantly and consistently covering someone who refuses to make better choices? To expect limitless covering without accepting personal responsibility, produces a selfish spirit.

You can always tell when a selfish spirit has entered the marriage because it produces a double standard! Never mind how I forgave and covered your transgressions, and now when you have to cover me in my transgressions, you can't find it in your heart.

The marriage goes to another level when you cover me, and I cover you. The Lord's prayers suggest we are forgiven as we forgive. When you cover me and I cover you, we present a united front to stand against the enemy. The Bible also declares, a house divided against itself cannot stand. So, as we make a commitment to cover one another, we produce a marriage that will stand the test of time. This is essential when raising a family and building a legacy.

No Longer Committed to The Marriage

The minute your spouse walks away from Christ is when you know that they are not committed to the marriage. This is major because if the relationship to Christ is lost, there is no foundation to stand on. Where there is no commitment, there is no covering. In this situation, you have to be the first line of defense, and know it's a job for God to do. Not you.

When Covering has Turned into Enablement

This is a hard one because this is our spouse and we did say until death do us part. The two have become one; however, if my covering has turned into enablement we are in dangerous territory. This is when your spouse is not becoming better and their expectations to be rescued has exceeded your capacity to cover them.

There is only so much a person can take! When we are having more bad days than good, and when things are falling apart, my capacity to hold everything and everyone will cave. To expect an unlimited supply of covering with no sign that it's becoming better will produce bitterness. It's here that a decision has to be made. Do I stay in this vicious cycle of covering you and you're not becoming better, or I shift gears and move so that I can experience the season of celebration I know God has for me!

Once you have mastered the importance of covering one another, you can have effective collaboration. Let's explore more in the next chapter.

Part V: Collaboration

9

Collaboration

Webster defines the word Collaboration as the action of working with someone to produce or create something.

I've seen in marriages an attitude that's all about me, myself and I. This is how much I make, this is what I bring to the table, this is my credit score. You moved into my house, you're driving my car. With this attitude, you're not going to build very much.

If you're building everything with just your two hands, you only have the capacity to do and hold what you can by yourself. It's not until you understand that two is better than one, that you'll grow in collaboration.

When I take my two hands and add the hands of my spouse, that's four hands! And together we can accomplish anything, as long as we learn to collaborate. This is the mechanism that produces celebration throughout a relationship.

In this section we'll talk about effective collaboration, the beauty of collaboration, introduce the antithesis of it, and how to avoid it.

Effective Collaboration

The Three H's of Collaboration

In order to effectively collaborate, you must have what we call the three H's of Collaboration, which is honor, humility and honesty. Let's explore each one.

Honor

Honor simply means to highly respect someone or to hold someone in great esteem. When you honor someone, you fully respect them in every sense of the word. Honor is a lost art in marriages today. Many people who are getting married have no real concept of what it means to honor your spouse. When you honor your spouse, you respect them on the highest level. In the world in which we live in today, we hold onto our honor because honoring you means I'm devaluing or dishonoring myself. The world would suggest that honoring you places the light on the honoree while the person who is doing the honoring looks weak.

When you honor someone, it is not a sign of weakness. Honor is a sign of respect, reverence and strength. When you honor your spouse, it sends a signal to the world that they hold a special and significant place in your life. When you honor your spouse, it sends a signal to the world that God loves you so much He has allowed you to share your life with someone worthy of your respect, even if they're not in your presence. We're living in a day where society wants us to believe we can do whatever we want, with whomever we want, how we want and live any kind of way, even in the sanctity of marriage. I mean after all, what my spouse doesn't know won't hurt them. So we go on girls trips and guy trips and we leave our honor back at home. In case you didn't know, honor has a passport, frequent flyer miles, and you can take honor wherever you go. As a matter of fact, the true test of honor is when you can be honorable in the absence of your spouse.

Honor is a sign of respect, and where there is respect, you can expect a reward. As we stated earlier, the church is the bride of Christ and Christ loved his bride so much that he died for it. We as the church should always honor Christ in our lives, we should always respect and reverence Christ and hold him in highest esteem! When we do we can expect a reward. The Bible declares that one day, Christ is coming back for his church and we will be caught up to meet him in the air. Just as we should honor Christ, we should honor our spouses in marriage! When we do so, God will bless our marriage in ways we can't even imagine. When your children get older, they will rise up and call you blessed, long after you're gone and your grandchildren will speak well of your name. That's your reward, that's how powerful we should honor our spouses.

Humility

This is a tough one, especially for men, because we have been taught to be strong. As a man we have been taught you don't cry, figure it out, pick up the pieces and keep moving. As a man, humility can be viewed as a weakness. So with all of those biases ingrained in our psyche, we approach marriage with that mindset. We must be strong, steadfast, and we can't show any signs of weakness. My working definition of what it means to operate in humility is to suggest that humility is the absence of pride. In other words, pride and humility cannot live in the same space. Pride suggests I did this or we are because of me. Where there is pride, there is no humility. We must be careful operating in the spirit of pride, because the Bible declares pride goes before a fall. If two will ever become one and reach new heights, humility must be evident in the marriage.

How do we walk in humility?

Personal admission

Admit it! Let's face it, we need our partners help. As we said before, you cannot allow pride to keep the marriage from walking in the fullness of promise. You may experience some success on your own, but you will never see the full manifestation of what the marriage could be doing it on your own. So it is here that you must admit, I need my partner's help. When you have the courage to admit it, you're now operating with the spirit of humility.

Purposely seeking your partners advice

When you are walking in humility, and you admit that you can't do it on your own, who better to seek advice or council from than your partner. In a marriage, when you win, the marriage wins. It's a sign of admission you don't have all the answers. When you seek your partners advice, you may find out where you're coming up short and how your partner may be able to supply.

Partnership ascension

Have you ever heard the phrase you get more bees with honey than you would ever get with vinegar? When you have the courage to admit that you need help and when you have the consciousness to seek your partner's advice, you can expect your marriage to ascend. We previously said that two is better than one. It's an amazing picture when you are working together to achieve one common goal. Your marriage will go to another level because you're covered on all sides. The world opens up to us all the more because we have a spirit of collaboration and it benefits our marriage and our family.

Honesty

When I was growing up, my mother always said, honesty is the best policy. When you are collaborating in a marriage, you have to be honest with one another. As a matter of fact, if you can't be honest with your spouse, who can you be honest with?

William Shakespeare said, "to thy own self be true." If you are not honest with yourself, you will try to do it all. It will require a spirit of honesty to admit that you can't do it all alone. Two is always better than one. Many married couples miss the mark because they privately pursue their own destiny even though they are partners in a marriage. You have your stuff and I have my stuff. You have your money and I have my money. Or you have your credit report, I have my credit report and even though we have the same goal, we never reach it because we failed to collaborate.

Honesty will help you to come to the conclusion I can't do it all by myself. This is a very vulnerable position to be in, because now you have to admit to your spouse I need your help. The world has decided if you asked for help you are weak, but as men, we must understand that the wife has been created and designed to be our helpers. That's why the Bible calls them help meets. They operate at their optimum level when they are helping us bring our vision to pass, that's why the Bible declares when a man finds a wife, he finds a good thing and he obtains favor with God. When you operate in the spirit of honesty, under the umbrella of collaboration, you move closer to your destiny. You get halfway by yourself but with your spouse, you can go further and dream bigger.

You also have to be honest and be able to identify each other's strengths and weaknesses. You can't get caught up in your feelings and emotions because then it can turn into competition. We recently shared our experience with collaboration in the kitchen. My husband's strength is that he is a wonderful cook. He cooks some of the best dishes and it is absolutely amazing! We often prefer his cooking rather than eating out. Although he is a fantastic cook, he's not the best at cleaning. That's where I come in. In order to make sure we have a good meal without a huge mess, I clean up as he's cooking. In spite of times past, I accept the fact that as the woman of the house, I'm not the best cook and that's okay. I don't get in my feelings and try to cross into his lane. Instead, I do what I do best to help, which is clean. His good food plus a clean kitchen equals a very good night.

My husband is more in the limelight, talking and ministering to others, while I'm behind the scenes as more of a critical thinker and planner. When he's preaching, I'm in the audience supporting him and making sure the service is going smoothly.

This turns into an amazing dance! Being able to dance and balance each other out is a true sign of maturity. We've learned how to do this well, because again, being able to have each other's back is essential.

In truth, it's more powerful when I shine in my area, and he shines in his. Then when the two bright lights come together, we can make whatever project it is great because of our ability to support each other in our own unique way. This is our reality and it works of us. Find what works for you and work it!

10

The Benefits and Beauty of Collaboration in The Family

In the world today, whether it's a job, ministry or a business venture, we're able to survive hard times because of collaboration. Had we not embraced working together, we would not have made it through bringing in our mother to live with us, the loss of our child, the birth of a ministry, losing a home and so much more. Collaborating as a unit has been imperative to our ability to build something great for the betterment of the family.

This skill isn't just for married couples, it even applies to our children. We have a puppy, and our oldest daughter often gets aggravated that her younger siblings don't do their part. It's a wonderful lesson where we can teach the importance of working together. They surely manipulated and collaborated to get the puppy, and now they get to learn the value of hard work. You wanted it, so it's up to you to make it work!

Learn how to collaborate and you'll enhance those skills inside and outside a strong family unit at home. If not, the enemy of collaboration steals from the productivity and joy of your marriage.

Every family dynamic may be different than ours; however, the final result is the same. When you collaborate, you win. We nourish and support each other and it's a beautiful work! We sharpen each other's weaknesses and build each other's strengths so that the family wins.

The Antithesis of Collaboration

When we talk about collaboration, at its core, we're talking about two different worlds coming together to make one. Everything that we've learned, how we were raised, our personalities, they all come together to make one life in marriage. Compromise becomes critical to do this properly.

Today, you may have one view and one way of doing things, but it's through collaboration that you're able to benefit from a different perspective. If we're not able to do this, what are the pitfalls and dangers of not collaborating as a unit?

For one, you won't experience the joy of a new viewpoint or diversity in ways of living life. If you're not collaborating, it's like having dark and limited tunnel vision. It can be intimidating for people, and even risky to be open to another's view or way of doing things. We may not know what's on the other side of letting go and trusting another person, but we encourage you to explore different things in life and understand there are going to be unknowns. The key to remember is that fear doesn't have to rule you.

Release Control and Let Go

Most of us are used to being in control. It takes effort and faith to relax and collaborate with another person, trusting they may have a better way. Especially when you're used to a certain way you like things to be done, or even more so if you are someone who hates not knowing how things are going to work out.

To experience the new and to benefit from collaboration, you have to be able to let go of the control and let your guard down. Allow the spirit of compromise to be instituted, which will make releasing that control easier to do. When you release control and work to-gether, you give your spouse time to shine from behind the stage to the spotlight. It's tough to do, but worth it. Plus, it's better to be sharing the stage with someone instead of being the only one. Let go of the control and operate in a spirit of compromise.

Conclusion

11

Celebrate

We can honestly say, after experiencing the trials and tribulations of life, implementing the principles throughout this book has definitely strengthened our marriage and we are now in a season of celebration!

There's a process of development before the fullness of celebration. You can't just skip to this part. Skipping this process is one of the biggest mistakes we made early on in marriage. We want you to know and understand that there's a process to this. "After you have suffered a while, He'll restore, confirm, strengthen and establish you."

We often want perfection and celebration without going through the process, and it just doesn't happen that way. Going through the process is what empowers couples that survive the trials and tribulations of life and stand strong after many years of marriage.

Whatever you do, don't fall for the fantasy of marriage with the house and kids. What you've dreamed of for your relationship is absolutely possible, and even more fulfilling with someone you're able to endure and grow stronger with.

Learn the lessons from what you're facing, because there's no reason to truly celebrate unless you've survived the chaos and come out better on the other side. You have survived and you've made it this far! You may not have a perfect marriage (no one does), but it's a strong one, and getting better and better, sweeter and sweeter as the years go by. It's worth celebrating every day.

If you work your marriage, celebration will be your portion. What is that work? Standing upon a strong foundation in Christ, being in commitment to each other, and covering the relationship in communication and collaboration.

It's Not How You Start, It's How You Finish

Great marriages are like everything else. It needs time. I remember when we first started out as I said earlier, we had very little. We had lots of love, lots of dreams, a big vision, but no money. When we got married, we were both 22 years old.

At 22, we had already been dating for seven years, so we had a good start. We just needed more time. Anything great requires time. It may not look like greatness in the beginning but over time, it will develop into greatness. Someone asked me how does my make mac & cheese turn out so good? The truth of the matter is, you can buy a box of macaroni and cheese and have it ready in about 10 minutes. It will only be mac & cheese, but it will not be great mac & cheese. Great mac & cheese needs time to bake and simmer. It's a process!

Many marriages end in divorce because of lack of time. Any marriage celebrating 20, 30, and 40 years has the same thing in common: it has stood the test of time. You can't expect a great marriage in the first two years. Many marriages will start strong, but they will not stay strong. We challenge you to start out strong and stay strong throughout the years so that you can finish strong.

The Joy in the Journey

Many assume that marriage is a sprint when it is a marathon or a journey. A sprint is a race where you get to the finish line, quick, fast, and in a hurry. As a matter of fact, when you are in a sprint, there is a prize to the winner who finishes the fastest. Down through the years, we have seen many marriages start out fast not realizing marriage is a marathon. One of the biggest mistakes a runner makes in a marathon is mismanaging pace. When you are running a marathon, you have to be cognizant of the pace you are running. As a matter of fact, the Bible declares the race is not given to the swift nor the battle to the strong, the race is given to the one that can endure until the end.

When you are married, it is a journey and there will be ups and downs. There will be twists and turns. People will be born and people will die. Even with the trials of life, find the joy in the journey. Many marriages will get defeated, distracted, and discouraged because they can't see the finish line in the journey. We want to suggest to you on this journey of marriage, don't overlook the joy that is in the journey.

Don't Allow the Next Moment to Hinder the Now Moment

Oftentimes we get so busy on what's next that we don't take a moment to breathe in the now. As we conquer one mountain, we move to the next. As a matter of fact, our culture has a slogan, "No

Days Off.". We want to challenge the slogan and suggest to you, Don't miss the Now Moment chasing the Next Moment. The Bible declares "Weeping may endure for a night but Joy comes in the morning." After you have endured a night or a season of weeping, take a moment and bask in the joy of the moment. Take a deep breath and look back and see where God has brought you from.

P.Diddy says " The sun don't always shine forever but since we're here we might as well shine together." There will definitely be some dark days, there will be some sad days, and there will be days where you will want to throw in the towel. When you encounter these kind of days, draw from the good days you've had, the moments that took your breath away and the days you laughed until you cried. Visualize the moment you saw each other standing at the altar, the moments you and your spouse have created together and find the joy inside the journey.

Celebrate Small Wins

As I write this, my mind goes back to the early years of our marriage where we were so focused and steadfast on getting a house, which would be considered a huge win, we missed a lot of other moments we could have celebrated along the way. I often have this conversation with my wife and ask what were we thinking? Why didn't we travel more? Why didn't we take more risks? Why didn't we go to Jerusalem, Hawaii, or Rome when it was just the two of us?

We were so focused on scoring a big victory, we didn't count the small ones. There were moments when we received promotions on our job and had other achievements, but we were so focused on our future goal that we didn't celebrate the now moment. There were moments where we were recognized for the work we were doing in the community but it took a back seat to the goal at hand. Seasons come and seasons go. When you look back, you don't want to live in the regret of what could have been. Celebrate it all!

Marriage Still Works

For us, divorce was never an option, and there has never been a Plan B. We know that's a cliche statement, but it's the truth.

Like the Hokey-Pokey song, you have to put your whole self into this if you want to celebrate longevity in your marriage. It can't be just your right arm or your left foot in. It has to be your whole self, and for many couples this is scary.

It's why they have a back-up plan in place, and a mindset that says, "If things don't go the way I want it to, then I'm going somewhere else." The Bible says it's the little foxes that spoil the vine, and we've had to wrestle with some little things that began to eat away at our relationship before they became major things.

We had to work through it together and didn't realize at the time that we were putting the principles in place that we shared with you in this book.

We are looking forward to the next 22 years of marriage and know it's going to get sweeter. As our children get older and begin attending middle school, then high school, that will be a new experience for us and we are looking forward to it!

We can declare with confidence that because our foundation is solid with Christ at the center, we are able to stand strong together, no matter the changing seasons and phases of life. The best is yet to come!

Remember anything worth having is worth fighting for, so stay in the good fight of faith. The greater the challenge, the greater the celebration. Know in your heart that marriage still works, if you work it. We hope this book empowers and inspires you to do your work.

Acknowledgements

We would like to acknowledge our parents and all of our family and friends for your amazing love and support. We would have never made it to 22 years without you all.

A special thanks to our church family. Thank you for allowing us to serve you and speak life into you week after week.

About The Authors

Nelson and Ayeisha White have a heart for people and their mission is to love people until they begin to love themselves, to lift them up out of what they are in and point them to Jesus and to speak life over them to push them to becoming the best version of themselves.

In a world where many have given up on marriage, lost hope that it will ever happen or believe that marriage can't be fixed, Nelson and Ayeisha are on a mission to Reignite Passion, Restore the Power of Marriage and to Remind the world that Marriage Still Works!

Nelson and Ayeisha are the founders of The House of Hope Praise Ministries in Clinton, MD. and they serve as the Senior Pastor and First Lady. They are middle school sweethearts and have been happily married for 22 years! Nelson and Ayeisha reside in White Plains, MD and they have 3 beautiful children Autumn, Aubrey and Noah.

www.ingramcontent.com/pod-product-compliance
Lightning Source LLC
Chambersburg PA
CBHW051446150726

48000CB00005B/2274